The closeness of God

CARMELITE MONASTERY

LIBRARY

SARANAC LAKE, N.Y.

*Also by Ladislaus Boros
and published by The Seabury Press*

ANGELS AND MEN

CHRISTIAN PRAYER

HIDDEN GOD

THE MYSTERY OF DEATH

PAIN AND PROVIDENCE

The closeness of God

Ladislaus Boros

Translated by David Smith

A Crossroad Book
The Seabury Press • New York

1978
The Seabury Press
815 Second Avenue
New York, N.Y. 10017

Originally published as
Der nahe Gott
© Matthias-Grünewald-Verlag 1971

This translation
© Search Press Limited 1977

All rights reserved. No part of this book may be reproduced,
stored in a retrieval system, or transmitted, in any form or by
any means, electronic, mechanical, photocopying,
recording, or otherwise, without the written permission of
The Seabury Press.

Library of Congress Catalog Card number: 78-52262
ISBN: 0-8164-2175-7
Printed in the United States of America

Contents

Foreword

This book originated in conversation about the main theme and associated topics for a day of meditation. My aim was essentially to let those attending be converted, turn inwards and go straight to the heart of Christian faith. No theological or philosophical knowledge was presupposed. The talks were for people who knew that they were not yet completely at home in their lives; people with questions rather than problems. They were for those in search of security.

We are all looking for a home and this individual quest can be seen in cosmic terms as the world's longing for glory. Our conversion, our turning inwards, is our personal sign of the world's desire ultimately to return to the glory of God. This return is evoked in Psalm 87. The author describes all mankind making a pilgrimage to Jerusalem and arriving in great joy at the gates of the city. We should remember, when we meditate on this psalm, that Jerusalem was for those people (who represent all mankind) the very centre of their existence. It was a vision that threw light on everything. The images of the psalm contain an essential truth: that it is man's destiny to meet God at the end of time and to be united with him in holiness. Now, mankind is awake to this destiny and is standing at the gates of the holy city and singing: 'All my springs are in you' (Ps 87. 7).

If we are to be truly converted and turn inwards and back to God, we must learn to know God as the source of our life. I think this normally takes place in prayer. But what is prayer? When I speak of prayer in this book, I mean something quite fundamental — opening one's life

to God. Our whole being is, of course, already essentially
open to God at all times. God is the centre from which
all our activity stems. Augustine once said of this centre,
our heart, that it was always restless until it found rest
in God. The restlessness of our hearts is therefore already
a revelation in itself, a sign that the Holy Spirit is praying
in our hearts 'with sighs too deep for words' (Rom 8. 26).
In this sense prayer is a basic event in our lives.

Man is therefore praying all the time to God in the
depths of his soul. Or rather, he does not pray, but
prayer is in him. He is taken towards God in prayer.
Whenever we pray explicitly, all that is happening is that
we are being driven consciously towards God. Prayer, as
it were, forms the undercurrent of the movement of our
soul. When we pray, all that we are doing – and all that
we ought to be doing – is to let ourselves be driven more
and more completely towards God. It is the function of
the Holy Spirit to let loose a storm in us that will, so to
speak, impel us to pray explicitly. As soon as we begin
to pray, our turning inwards and back to God has already
been accomplished. We should, however, be careful to
remember that this can only take place in recollectedness
and serenity. Tension has no part to play in prayer. The
exercises contained in this book are therefore only to be
taken as suggestions. They will also only be understood
by those who try to follow the paths indicated in their
personal lives.

Remember, too, that every meditation has to begin in
solitude or rather by withdrawing into yourself. It is
there that the ultimate glory is to be found. Being
driven towards God, we go down to the depths of our
being. Turning inwards and back to God is our best way
of realizing our longing for him. To achieve this, we
have to be recollected, alone and serene.

God speaks to us

Turning back to God and inwards in order to fulfil our longing for God's presence is not easy these days. In this chapter I shall try to outline the basic elements of being addressed by God.

An image from the Bible
I have chosen a rather unusual course here. I have taken the Book of Jonah as a guide for our thoughts. Man's struggle with and for God is presented in a very pure form in this book. Anyone who has heard or read the story of Jonah finds it difficult to forget its deeply human impact. It is a basically simple account of the events in the life of a man who was addressed by God. At first he refused to accept his mission from God. Later, after he had accepted it and carried it out success-fully, he was 'angry enough to die' (Jon 4. 9). Let us now look at this well-known story and its interpretation.

The story
'Now the word of the Lord came to Jonah' (1. 1). A man heard the word of God, commanding him to go to Nineveh, the capital of Assyria. He was to preach to the inhabitants of the city, telling them that the God of Israel intended to destroy them.

Clearly, that was not a pleasant task. In the first place, the Assyrians were in no sense friendly towards the Jews. What is more, a man proclaiming news like that might well be treated badly. So 'Jonah rose to flee to Tarshish from the presence of the Lord' (1. 3). His only thought was to escape from God. So he fled to Tarshish — for the Jews, the end of the world. Flight from God to the end of the world.

Jonah was essentially a practical man; he thought in concrete terms, and planned his flight in detail. First he went to Joppa, a Philistine port on the Mediterranean coast, to look for a ship going to Tarshish. He found one surprisingly quickly, paid his fare and went on board. At once he looked for a quiet corner inside the ship and lay down to rest after the exertions of the journey — his so far very successful flight from God. The sailors set sail and they set off for Tarshish. Everything had passed off very easily. Perhaps a little too easily.

Then, 'the Lord hurled a great wind upon the sea, and there was a mighty tempest on the sea, so that the ship threatened to break up' (1. 4). The sailors first threw all kinds of objects that were in the ship into the sea, in order to lighten the load on board. While all this was going on, however, Jonah was asleep. Obviously angry, the captain accused him: 'What do you mean, you sleeper? Arise and call upon your God! Perhaps that God will give a thought to us, that we do not perish!' (1. 6).

In the meantime, the ship's crew had thought of a solution. 'Let us cast lots,' they said, 'that we may know on whose account this evil has come upon us' (1. 7). The lot fell on Jonah and at once something very remarkable happened. Jonah immediately confessed what he was doing and why he was doing it and asked the sailors to throw him into the sea. The men were at first reluctant to place Jonah so entirely at the mercy of the storm and 'rowed hard to bring the ship back to land, but they could not, for the sea grew more and more tempestuous against them' (1. 13). They then realized that it was God's will that Jonah should be delivered up to the storm and threw him overboard. And at once 'the sea ceased from its raging' (1. 15).

The waves closed over Jonah. He was whirled about in the deep, brought up to the surface and tossed around on the swell. In his distress he prayed to the Lord and the words of his prayer are without equal in the whole of the Old Testament (2. 2-9). The first part of the story ends simply and astonishingly: 'The Lord appointed a great fish to swallow up Jonah. And Jonah was in the belly of the fish for three days and three nights . . . And the Lord spoke to the fish, and it vomited out Jonah upon the dry land' (1. 17; 2. 10).

The second part begins: 'The word of the Lord came to Jonah the second time, saying, "Arise, go to Nineveh, that great city, and proclaim to it the message that I tell you" ' (3. 2). In the meantime, Jonah's experience had taught him something about his God, so he 'arose and went to Nineveh' at once (3. 3).

In his sermon, he threatened the people: 'Yet forty days, and Nineveh shall be overthrown!' (3. 4). But the Ninevites' reaction to his words was different from what Jonah had expected and 'believed God' (3. 5). The king of Nineveh published a decree throughout the city: 'Let man and beast be covered with sackcloth and let them cry mightily to God; let everyone turn from his evil way and from the violence which is in his hands' (3. 8). Stylistically this whole passage leaves a lot to be desired, but God looks into the heart of man and not at the literary expression. When he 'saw what they did, how they turned from their evil way, God repented of the evil which he had said he would do to them and he did not do it' (3. 10).

Jonah left the city to seek refuge from the impending disaster. He stayed at a safe distance for several days, ready to watch the destruction of Nineveh. As he sat waiting, 'to the east of the city,' in a shelter he had made himself, 'till he should see what would become of the city' (4. 5), the Lord let him know that the city would not after all be destroyed.

This made Jonah angry and he began to quarrel with God. His prophesying was completely wasted and his sufferings had been in vain. He could not bear it. 'Is not this what I said when I was yet in my country? That is

why I made haste to flee to Tarshish; for I knew that
thou art a gracious God and merciful, slow to anger, and
abounding in steadfast love, and repentest of evil' (4. 2).
He reproached his God and finally pleaded with him: 'O
Lord, take my life from me, for it is better for me to die
than to live' (4. 3).

Jonah was deeply annoyed and God left him in his
annoyance. Secretly, however, he was planning to give
Jonah a remarkable lesson. During the night, he made a
tree grow miraculously over Jonah so that he was shaded
from the burning sun. Jonah was 'glad because of the
plant' (4. 6). From then on, he slept and slept. He must
really have been a tremendous sleeper, because he was
able to sleep in any situation — even during a raging
storm at sea! Now he slept for a whole day, a night and
the following day.

In the meanwhile, however, God sent miraculous
worms, 'which attacked the plant, so that it withered'
(4. 7). The sun began to beat down on Jonah's head and
he awoke under the withered tree with a headache. He
was 'angry enough to die' (4. 9). The story of the
prophet ends with God's words. 'You feel miserable',
God assured Jonah, 'because I have taken the tree away
from you. Now you can imagine how I felt when I
decided to destroy the great city of Nineveh, where
more than a hundred and twenty thousand people live'.

So much for the story. What, then, does it mean? If
we are to understand fully the meaning of any biblical
account, we have to know its 'literary genre'. It is quite
obvious that the story of Jonah is not one of the so-
called historical books of the Bible. What is narrated
here never happened in fact.

Old Testament scholars have put forward at least five
arguments which prove convincingly that the author had
no intention of offering us historical or even biological
truth. Let us look briefly at each of these proofs. Firstly,
Jonah is only mentioned once elsewhere in the Bible
(2 Kg 14. 25) and must have lived at least five hundred

years before the prophetic book was written. Secondly, the city of Nineveh no longer existed at the time that the book of Jonah was written. It had been completely destroyed at least two hundred years before. Thirdly, there is no evidence, either in Jewish or in Assyrian sources, of the city and its ruler having been converted to Judaism. If such a conversion had ever taken place, the Jews at least would certainly have recorded it. Nothing, however, has ever come to light and the book of Jonah is the only place where this conversion is mentioned. Fourthly, there was no large city of the size of the 'Nineveh' of the book of Jonah (120,000 inhabitants!) in the whole of the ancient world. In addition to the number of inhabitants claimed, this 'Nineveh' is described in the third chapter of the book as 'an exceedingly great city, three days' journey in breadth' (3. 3). Compared with this, even London or New York would be a small provincial town.

Finally, there are certain zoological and botanical difficulties which cannot be explained very easily. In the first place, there is the fish that was able to swallow a man. In the second place, there is the statement that the man was able to spend three days and nights in the fish's belly and emerge unharmed. In the third place, there is the miraculous tree which grew so quickly and was killed so easily by the miraculous worm or worms.

These five difficulties are very important to bear in mind if we are to interpret the story of Jonah correctly. They show clearly that the author of the book did not want to give us historical, zoological or botanical information. Those who heard the story were no less well informed than we are, at least in matters concerning Jewish history. They certainly must have seen through the contradictions that we have outlined above. The author had to take their knowledge into account. Yet he left his story exactly as it is. Why? When we have found an answer to this question, we shall have the key that will open the door to our understanding of the story.

We have seen that the author did not aim to write a historical account. On the contrary, he deliberately used historical and biological details which were clearly untenable in order to raise his story above the level of the purely factual to that of the figurative and symbolic. We may say, quite simply, that when a writer in the East wanted to say something quite fundamental, he did not provide a description or a definition, but wrote a story, a myth or a legend.

In the book of Jonah, then, we are presented above all with the deep dialectical tension that results from an encounter between God and man. The author was anxious to avoid giving his readers (or listeners) the impression that his story was a report of genuine historical events; therefore he deliberately included elements which were historically obviously false. In the East, no one would put the book of Jonah on the shelf in his library marked 'History'. It would be classified under 'Poetry'. More precisely, the book is a poetic interpretation of man's existence.

As the principal human figure in the story, the prophet Jonah is vague in the extreme, because we know practically nothing at all about him. He is mentioned, as we have seen, once in the Old Testament (apart from the book of Jonah itself) and all that is said there is that he lived at the time of King Jeroboam II. Then, as we have also seen, he went, according to the author of the book, to a city that had been destroyed two centuries before. All the 'events' of the story are wrongly dated and there are several miracles. It is a myth, a legend, even a fairy story. It could just as well have begun with the words: 'Once upon a time . . . somewhere . . . someone . . .'

All the same, we are bound to ask: 'Where, then, is the revealed truth of this myth?' The answer is simple. What is said here in the form of a myth or legend is certainly a revelation of the relationship between God and man. It is a divine teaching about our sanctification.

In other words, in the story of Jonah, God himself has proposed a theme for meditation which will lead us to turn inwards and be converted. Let us accept this proposal and try to discover the truth of this theme for us.

Encounter with God

'Now the word of the Lord came to Jonah the son of Amittai, saying, "Arise, go to Nineveh, that great city" ' (Jon 1. 1-2). Even these introductory words contain a truth and we ought to reflect about it: God speaks to our souls. Or, to put this more precisely, my soul has depth because God speaks to it. This is the primary and fundamental fact of our spiritual life, indeed the beginning of that life. It means that God reveals himself to man.

The first letter of John opens with a remarkable sentence: 'That . . . which we have heard, which we have seen . . ., which we have looked upon and touched with our hands, concerning the word of life . . . we proclaim also to you' (1 Jn 1. 1-3). It is one of those many sentences belonging to God's revelation from which it is difficult to escape.

Anyone reading this sentence for the first time and not knowing that it came from the Bible and reflected the apostles' experience with Christ might imagine that a lover was describing his experience with another person whom he loved. Sentences of this kind do not become banal. They remain like seeds in our souls, ready to germinate. God has revealed himself to us, this sentence tells us. He has made himself known to our spirit and to our senses — we have heard, seen and touched him in our lives.

I will not speak, then, about an 'abstract' God here, but about the God who has spoken individually to each one of us and who has revealed himself personally to each of us. I will not speak either just of 'God', but of your God, of the God whom you have heard speaking in your soul, whom you have seen in the events of your life and whom you have touched in your moments of grace.

It is not important — at least at present — to ask
whether we can really give this God, that is, the God
who makes himself known to us personally, the name of
'God' as such. At present, all that we have to consider is
Jonah's experience. Jonah was suddenly confronted by
a God who made a total demand on him. He said something to him that concerned him alone.

We are often eager to keep hold of a personal encounter
with God and are curious to know how God succeeded
in penetrating to the very centre of our being. The
process by which we become conscious of God and his
dealings with us is very mysterious. It can be likened to
the formation of a stalactite or stalagmite, for it consists
of thousands and thousands of little drops. It is not
likely that we have ever grasped God as if he were the
conclusion to an abstract train of thought. More probably, we think of him as the central point of countless
allusions, connexions and relationships. As the heart of
our faithfulness, longing and love.

In his *Confessions* (7. 17), Augustine said that this
God could be grasped by our 'loving memory of God',
and his treatise is a record of a lifelong search for the
presence of God even in the simplest events in the
author's existence. I believe that this loving memory of
God is the fundamental exercise of all meditation. The
individual fragments of our experience of God may be
of little importance, like pieces of coloured glass. When
these pieces are put together, however, they may form a
mosaic like those found on the floors of Romanesque
cathedrals or Byzantine basilicas. We Christians should
therefore make a practice of piecing together the
apparently unimportant fragments of our experience of
God with the help of the unifying power of our loving
memory of God.

The moments of grace in our lives
Certain moments form the real heart of our existence.
At such times we feel ourselves to be very close to God.

When we experience this grace, we should always remember that God himself, clearly defined in radiant light, is standing in our presence. Such moments come to all of us. Sometimes it is even possible to remember the exact date and the time when God entered our lives like a flash of lightning. Let me give two examples of such moments of grace in the lives of two well-known Christians.

The first is Blaise Pascal's *Memorial*. It is clear from this carefully written and preserved document that it records one of the great moments in the life of the Christian philosopher. 'The year of grace 1654', the *Memorial* begins, 'Monday, 23 November, the day of Saint Clement, Pope and Martyr, and of others in the martyrology. The vigil of the feast of Saint Chrysogonus, Martyr, and others. From about half past ten in the evening until about half an hour after midnight. Fire. God of Abraham, God of Isaac, God of Jacob, not of the philosophers and scholars. Certainty, certainty, feeling, joy, peace. God of Jesus Christ . . .' This intimate and personal testimony describes an event in Pascal's life which divided what had gone before from what was to follow. It does not portray a vague feeling, an abstract view or a hesitant attitude. It speaks of history and decision.

My second example is taken from the life of Saint Augustine. The saint describes how he was travelling from Milan back to Africa with his mother and how they were breaking their journey in Rome. Monica was to die before they were able to resume the journey from the Roman port of Ostia. 'Not long before the day on which she was to leave this life . . .', Augustine writes, 'my mother and I were alone, leaning from a window which overlooked the garden in the courtyard of the house where we were staying at Ostia. We were waiting there after our long and tiring journey, away from the crowd, to refresh ourselves before our sea voyage . . . We were talking alone together and our conversation was serene and joyful . . . Our thoughts ranged over the whole compass of material things in their various degrees, up to the heavens themselves . . . Higher still we climbed . . . At length we came to our own souls and passed beyond them . . . And while we spoke of eternal wisdom, longing for it and straining for it with all the strength of our hearts, for one fleeting instant we reached and touched it' (*Confessions* 9, 10; trans. Pine-Coffin).

What Augustine is saying here is very similar to what Pascal says in the previous quotation. He even recalls the small details of the day at Ostia — for example, the very window at which he and his mother were standing when they became conscious of God's presence. In the lives of Augustine and Pascal, and, what is more, in our lives too, the 'memory of something loved' is the most important experience of all. We should preserve it, try to understand it and renew it again and again. This memory of God is surely our most precious possession.

I could give many other examples of this experience. There is, for instance, the great fire experience of Pierre Teilhard de Chardin, in which he was made suddenly conscious that the whole process of the evolution of the universe was sunk deep into the reality of Christ. There are also the great experiences of the Old Testament prophets.

But let us simply summarize what is common to them all. Suddenly, imperceptibly and quite unexpectedly, God breaks through to our soul. That is it, but there is also something else — God comes to us and is present with us, but he comes with a task. He came to Jonah and told him clearly: 'Arise, go to Nineveh' (Jon 1. 2). We may not recognize at once what it is that God wants. Or it may be that our task gradually emerges when we are close to God for a long time. But if we listen attentively, and listen within, we may hear what God is saying and know what he wants us to do.

God's images in us

These moments of light when God's grace crystallizes
in a direct experience are surrounded by a wider, darker
sphere of his constant presence. This is the environment
in which God's images can be seen. Those images are
extremely important in our spiritual lives. They show us
the forms in which God reveals himself personally to us.
It is therefore very important for each of us to ask
himself this question: What image rises up out of my
soul when I think about God? We should never try to
eliminate all images from our minds when we pray.
They are powerful signs and transform God's presence
into our own flesh and blood.

Each of us has his own favourite image of God. For
many of us it is light. We see God as the one who
enlightens and warms everything. Many saints have
experienced God's presence in this image of light and
great theologians have pointed to light as the sign of
God's activity in the world. We may, on the other hand,
see God as darkness. The essence of God himself has
been found by many Christians in the image of night, in
the mystery and intangibility of God. Other Christians
— and we may be among them — have found that the
image of height expresses God's presence perfectly. For
them, God is the one who transcends all things and who
cannot be reached unless the spirit is stretched to its
highest point. Then there are those who experience God
as concealed and unknowable in the depths of our being.
Their image is that of the abyss.

There is one more image of God that I would like to
develop a little more fully here, because it is one that
appeals to so many of us. That is the image — or rather
multiple image — of the wealth of creation. In his book
on God, Erich Przywara has written eloquently about
God's presence in the world: 'In the light wind of spring,
when the breezes sigh gently through young leaves as
soft and tender as children, when birth and new life are
visible everywhere and when young birds stretch their

wings and fly off into the endless blue sky . . . What is
the deeper meaning of this ecstasy of spring? Is it not a
premonition, pointing the way to a more perfect, eternal
spring? . . . to God, who, as Augustine said, is younger
than everything that is young and newer than everything
that is new. To God, eternal youth, eternal spring? Then
in the fulness, the overabundance of summer, the heavy
scent of the ripening fruit, the silence and restraint of
infinity . . . Is this not a foretaste of the silence and
fulness of an eternal summer, of God who is fulness
itself, but not satiety, the warmth and light of an eternal
midday sun, warming and enlightening without burning
and blinding, God the fruitfulness of eternity, the fruit
that lasts but does not decay? And in the cool, lonely
severity of autumn, that season that seems to be raised
far above man and free of any link with the physical
world, a time of hazy distances, heavy, cold mists and
veiled spectral shapes, when the whole of nature is tired,
silent and slowly dying . . . Is this not a foretoken of the
cool loneliness of God who is for ever and ever, God
who continues to exist unchanged and transcendent
above all that becomes and passes away? Is it not a sign
of the cool autumn of God's eternity?

'And then, finally, in winter, silent as the grave, all
nature living and breathing beneath the white, still snow
and the icy mantle of frost, and the soul of man listening
and saying nothing, inwardly waiting . . . Is this not a
message sent by a God who is unfathomable in his
silence, the quiet God who banishes the noise and
tempest of the world, God who waits eternal and still?'

There are, of course, many other images of God and
his presence in the soul of man. Some of us experience
God less in the wealth of our earth, his creation, and in
the powerful images evoked by the seasons than in the
void, the emptiness, the poverty of his inexpressible
nature. God is for such people a desert in which life is
drained of its strength and seeks solitude. A desert
without beauty, offering only dryness, silence and

severity. Very many of us, on the other hand, find God in the mystery of motherhood, fatherhood or childhood. God appears to some in the image of the judge, to others in the image of the beloved.

I could go on endlessly, listing image after image of God. But each one of us has the task of finding out for himself the image to which he reacts most fully and deeply in his own soul. For these images are the points of departure from which we go out to meet God personally.

God in the depth of our experiences
There is a third sphere in which God is close to us in an indistinct way. I would like to talk about this now.

Cardinal Manning once observed that all human experiences were fundamentally theological experiences. Karl Rahner has asked several pertinent questions about our moral attitude. We should try to answer them honestly. Have we ever been silent when we wanted to defend ourselves? Have we ever not spoken when we were unjustly treated? Have we ever forgiven someone without expecting or receiving any reward or acknowledgement? Have we obeyed another person, not because we had to and because it would have been unpleasant for us if we had not, but simply because of that mysterious, intangible and silent reality that is God and his will? Have we ever made a sacrifice, without thanks or recognition and even without that comfortable feeling of inner satisfaction? Have we ever been totally alone? Have we ever decided to do something, simply acting on the prompting of our conscience, to take action when no one would notice it or tell anyone that we had done it and when we would be acting entirely alone? Have we ever made a decision that was ours alone, Rahner asks — and here he touches on the infinite dimension of man's destiny — and involving a responsibility that would be ours for ever, even into eternity?

Rahner's questions now become more explicitly connected with man's relationship with God and he asks

whether we have ever tried to love God when we felt no
enthusiasm at all, when to love God was to deny ourselves, die to ourselves and enter an unfathomable and
totally unknown void where nothing was tangible and
everything seemed strange and meaningless? Have we
ever done something that could only be done with the
burning conviction that we are rejecting ourselves and
all that we have ever stood for? Have we done something
that seems to us and everyone else to be quite foolish?

Rahner summarizes all this in a final question — have
we ever been good to another person who gave no sign
at all of understanding what we had done and who gave
us no thanks, either explicitly or implicitly? Have we
ever done good and not even felt rewarded ourselves or
had the satisfaction of having behaved selflessly?

I would also conclude with this simple affirmation. If
we have done all this, then we shall have experienced
God in all these actions and attitudes as the deepest
reality. We shall have experienced him even if we have
never known him explicitly and have never been able to
name him as the one underlying all our good intentions
and acts.

God in the depth of our everyday experience

God is also present in other ways in our everyday human
experience. Although it is indistinct, his presence in
these ways in our daily lives is nonetheless profound,
real and very effective. He is, for example, present in
our experience of loneliness. We feel neglected, even
abandoned. We want to be loved by someone with a
truly human heart. We long to encounter another person,
to love someone else, to be two and not one. In this
experience of deep longing, we are working our way
towards God.

God is also present when we feel unfulfilled. This
experience can take many forms, but its usual expression
is boredom, sadness or dissatisfaction. We find the days
long and monotonous. Our work, which everyone else

seems to take for granted, and even our leisure-time activities, which others enjoy, leave us bitter and frustrated. We are disappointed with everything. Our wishes torment us and realizing them brings us no satisfaction. We experience more friction and conflict with other people and it hurts us more.

Each of us is conscious at some time or other in his life of this deep sense of being unfulfilled. But it is precisely this that is the presence of God in our soul. We are unfulfilled because we want so much, because we feel more, long for more and more and are conscious of so very much more; more than our own little life, our basically petty little life.

In this experience of being unfulfilled, however, what often preoccupies us at first is only the narrowness of our own heart and this makes us feel ashamed. We are ashamed of ourselves because our heart is cold and unloving, even though we know that we have within us an unlimited potential for happiness and love.

Yet even this feeling of shame can be turned to a positive end. The discovery of the emptiness and self-deception of our life makes us profoundly aware of the great determination and energy with which we have devoted ourselves to the pursuit of our own self. What, then, is positive in this? It is that the depth of our own shame makes us open to receive the one who is coming to meet us, the one who planted the seed of this longing for pure love in our heart. We are open to receive God himself.

If we look patiently, we can discover God's presence again and again in every truly human act of our existence. To find him, all we have to do is to look at our own happiness, our sad experiences, our acts of love, our own imperfections, our constant longings and the ways in which we carry out our little responsibilities every day, faithfully or perhaps sometimes reluctantly. In all these acts and experiences, God comes to meet us. He is never, in fact, very far from us.

I should like to conclude this short and very imperfect account of the ways in which God is present in us by pointing out that there are one or two even more important places where God can be encountered. One of these is Holy Scripture. The real task should then begin at once or at the latest in the weeks and months to come. If we succeed, with the help of God's grace, in making visible a little of our own personal God, our small share in the great mosaic of the universal God, we shall have to step back from this image that we have of God in our soul, kneel down and say, quite simply: 'My God — my all'.

We have gained a fundamental insight into God and ourselves in this first consideration. It is that God speaks personally to each one of us and is close to each of us in a completely individual way. Let us therefore remember the one essential aspect of this consideration. It is this. Without knowing, man feels drawn by God. God is present for him in the mysterious depths of his being. His soul is entirely orientated towards God and he and God are very close to each other.

At the same time, however, it is also important to remember that whenever we want to say something of lasting value about our relationship with God, we always have at once to deny what we have said a moment before, almost as soon as we have said it. Yet God is always known at the end of any process that includes both statement and denial. When we deny what we have said, we do not find ourselves in a void and irresolute. The very opposite is true. Our denial enables us to gather the fruit of what we have previously said.

Let me apply this to what I have said in this chapter about God's presence. I said that man's soul is always striving to be as close as possible to God. I am bound to deny this and add that man is also inclined to move as far away from God as he can. Without knowing, he is in constant flight from God. These two — closeness to God and distance from God, being drawn by God and flight from him — are the essence of our relationship with God.

Man's flight from God

Man's distance from God! This is a burning question today and we must take care not to lose ourselves in idle speculation. How can this temptation be avoided? A solution is readily at hand — by returning to the story of Jonah.

In the story of the prophet, man's distance from God is expressed in three symbolic events. These are Jonah's flight to Tarshish, his sleeping during the storm at sea, and the distress of the crew caused by Jonah. Let us now see how the Bible deals with these three events.

The biblical story
In the first place, there is Jonah's flight to Tarshish. God said to Jonah: ' "Arise, go to Nineveh, that great city" ' (1. 2). God was close to Jonah and this closeness implied a task. What was Jonah's first reaction? 'Jonah rose to flee to Tarshish from the presence of the Lord' (1. 3). We have already seen that, for the Jews of that time, Tarshish was the end of the world. Jonah, then, was addressed by God, close to God and given a task by God. His reaction — like that of most of us — was to seek flight from God. To the end of the world.

Secondly, we find Jonah sleeping during the storm at sea. Sleep here is a symbol for forgetfulness of self and therefore forgetfulness of God. 'There was a mighty tempest on the sea, so that the ship threatened to break up. The mariners were afraid and each cried to his god . . . But Jonah had gone down to the inner part of the ship and had lain down and was fast asleep. So the captain came and said to him, "What do you mean, you sleeper?

Arise, call upon your god!" ' (1. 4-6).

The third element is the sailors' distress caused by Jonah. 'The Lord hurled a great wind upon the sea and there was a mighty tempest on the sea ... and the mariners threw the wares that were in the ship into the sea, to lighten it for them ... And they said, "What shall we do, that the sea may quiet down for us?" For the sea grew more and more tempestuous ... And they said to one another, "Come, let us cast lots, that we may know on whose account this evil has come upon us." So they cast lots, and the lot fell upon Jonah ... He said to them, "Take me up and throw me into the sea; then the sea will quiet down for you. For I know it is because of me that this great tempest has come upon you." So they took up Jonah and threw him into the sea; and the sea ceased from its raging' (1. 4-5, 7, 11-12, 15).

What had these poor sailors done for God to put them to the test in such a frightening way? Probably nothing at all or at least nothing very much. A law of life is expressed in this event — that each of us is inextricably linked with everyone else. Each individual is dependent on the community and the community depends on its individual members. We are connected with our fellow men in good fortune and bad. All of us become remote from God if one of us deliberately removes himself from God. The individual's distance from God leads to the community's distance from God.

We shall now look more closely at each of these three symbols in turn, examine the whole question of man's distance from God in the light of these symbols, and then turn to the meaning of that distance from God for ourselves.

Flight from God

What is our first reaction as soon as we are addressed by God? We react as Jonah did — almost involuntarily, we shrink back. Flight is an essential aspect of our attitude towards God. We should try to understand and accept this, because it would help us to appreciate why there is such a powerful and at times so oppressive conviction of distance from God in the world today. On the one hand, man is constantly being drawn to God. He longs to be in the presence of this irresistibly fascinating reality. On the other hand, however, even while he is longing for God, he also shrinks back from him. God is also the incomprehensible and terrifying reality. He both attracts and fills with awe.

Theologians would say — correctly — that man could not run away from God if God did not constantly withdraw himself from us. God's flight from man is the prerequisite for man's flight from God. God's presence consists, then, of distance and closeness. Hölderlin once wrote in a poem entitled *Meno's lament for Diotima* that a friendly presence had to be near him from afar. He also said, in the first version of his *Patmos*, that God is near and difficult to grasp. The closeness of God does not become really near to us until he is distant. We experience his closeness in a continuous exodus. This 'going out' brings distance and sorrow.

It brings sorrow. God can make us unhappy. There is no greater unhappiness than the unhappiness that God causes his friends. I once asked an old Carthusian what he had experienced in sixty years of denying himself and seeking God in his monastery. He replied: 'Sixty years of abandonment'. God is nameless and is always withdrawing himself. Gregory of Nyssa's hymn gives us an insight into this aspect of God:

'You are beyond everything. Is this all that can be said about you? Is there any hymn that can do justice to you? No word can express you. What, then can we say? You are so far above our understanding. You are inexpressible. Everything that can be expressed has come from you. You are unthinkable, because everything that can be thought has come from you. All creatures, whether they speak or whether they are silent, proclaim you. All creatures, whether they think or whether they

are irrational, bear witness to your glory. The longing
and sighing of the universe rise up to you. Everything
that exists prays to you. Every creature that lives in
your world sends up a hymn of silence to you. Everything
that remains in existence remains because of you. You
enable the universe to continue to move. You are the
real goal of all things. You are all things. And yet you
are none of them. Not even in their totality. You are no
single being. You are not even the totality of all beings.
All names belong to you. But what should I call you?
You cannot be named. Will any heavenly spirit ever be
able to break through the mists that conceal your
heaven? You are beyond and above everything! This is
perhaps all that can be said about you.'

It is a terrifying experience to look at God rising up
above us to endless heights like an enormous cliff and
falling down below us into unfathomable depths. It is
not even thinkable that this gigantic block that is God
does not exist. We gaze at him from the edge of our
existence, but he has no edge from which it is possible
to fall into nothingness. He is not even surrounded by
nothingness. That would be intolerable for him.

What, then, is the value of the names that we give to
God? Does it have any meaning to try to name him? It
sometimes seems almost absurd — one might say 'mean-
ingfully absurd' — to name God. Our names for God
provide us with a sense of direction. They at least point
in the direction we have to go if we are to overcome
ourselves and our own ideas about God, to learn anything
at all about the reality of God and to recognize that
everything that we already believe with regard to that
reality is totally inadequate. It is, for instance, better to
call God 'wisdom' than to deny that he is wise, even
though the word 'wisdom' always sounds silly, even
ridiculous, on our lips. Again, it is better to call God a
Spirit, even though the word 'Spirit' has a childish
sound as soon as we utter it. One final comment — it is
disturbing to see a man struggling with God himself

when he is at the same time both close to and distant from God.

Symbols for the closeness and distance of God

Let us turn away from the story of Jonah for a while and look at some other biblical examples of the extremely close connexion between man's flight or distance from God and God's closeness or revelation.

The first is the Old Testament account of God's revelation of himself to Moses in the burning bush (Exod 3. 1-6). This incident forms part of one of the most decisive events in the religious history of mankind. Moses had left Pharaoh's court in Egypt and fled into the desert. He had married the daughter of a nomadic prince and had been accepted as a member of the tribe. He had been put in charge of the shepherds. According to reports, he himself looked after sheep. Nowadays, we think of shepherds as having rather lowly work. At the time of Moses, however, it was an important function and shepherds were honoured. Kings were called shepherds. God himself was glad to be called a shepherd.

On this particular occasion, Moses had taken his flock to a different grazing ground — that was common practice among shepherds. Eventually he reached a mountainous region where the so-called 'mountain of God' was. He was surrounded by familiar things — the holy mountain, the sheep and the silence of the desert. Suddenly, however, all these things ceased to be familiar and ordinary and Moses was seized by an unfamiliar and extraordinary experience.

'The angel of the Lord', the biblical account tells us (and we understand by this, of course, that this is God himself), 'appeared to him in a flame of fire out of the midst of a bush; and he looked and lo, the bush was burning, yet it was not consumed. And Moses said, "I will turn aside and see this great sight, why the bush is not burnt". And when the Lord saw that he turned aside to see, God called to him out of the bush, "Moses,

Moses!" And he said, "Here I am". Then God said, "Do not come near; put off your shoes from your feet, for the place on which you are standing is holy ground". And he said, "I am the God of your father, the God of Abraham, the God of Isaac and the God of Jacob" '.

What is perhaps the most important sentence of all, at least for us here, follows now: 'And Moses hid his face, for he was afraid to look at God' (Exod 3. 6). The closeness of God was for Moses an unapproachable distance. God's glory was a deathly strangeness. Moses' experience of God — and ours — can only be understood in the light of this contrast, that revelation is at the same time a concealment. Light is at the same time darkness, beauty is withdrawal and when God is present he is hidden from sight.

A second remarkable event is Elijah's vision on the same mountain hundreds of years later (1 Kg 19. 9-14). Elijah, who was one of the greatest of the prophets, had, during the reign of King Ahab and his wife Jezebel, to fight against a wall of indifference to faith, hardness of heart and blood lust that had been built up in the land. His life was entirely devoted to the service of God. God's spirit burnt inside him, raised him high above his fellow men and filled him with an energy that was beyond that of ordinary men.

Now, however, he felt at the end of his strength. He lay like an exhausted animal in the desert and longed for death. But an angel touched him as he slept and he went forward. He had to escape from Jezebel. At last he found a place to hide in one of the caves in Horeb, the mountain of God. An astonishing incident took place there, as he stood at the entrance of the cave: 'A great and strong wind rent the mountains and broke in pieces the rocks, but the Lord was not in the wind; and after the wind an earthquake, but the Lord was not in the earthquake; and after the earthquake a fire, but the Lord was not in the fire; and after the fire a still small voice. And when Elijah heard it, he wrapped his face in his mantle and went out and stood at the entrance of the cave'.

A great deal is contained in this mysterious event, but what is important for us here and now is that it too points to the fact that, when we are very close to God, we experience his closeness as distance and his presence is hidden from us. God seized hold of Elijah and at the same time remained inaccessible and withdrawn.

Our third example is the story of the calling of the prophet Isaiah (Is 6. 1-8). The vision is described in these words: 'In the year that King Uzziah died I saw the Lord sitting upon a throne, high and lifted up; and his train filled the temple. Above him stood the seraphim; each had six wings; with two he covered his face, with two he covered his feet and with two he flew . . . And I said: "Woe is me! For I am lost . . . for my eyes have seen the King, the Lord of hosts'. Rilke once described these seraphim (in one of his *Duinese Elegies*) as those who had been blessed first, God's spoilt children, the high mountain ridges of the dawn of creation, the pollen of God's blossom, joints of light, corridors, stairs, thrones, rooms of essential life, shields of delight and tumults of delighted feeling. Yet even these seraphim, these glowing torches of God's love, experienced God as concealment, for they concealed themselves when God revealed himself to them.

Fourthly, I should like to point to a characteristic of God's revelation that occurs in several biblical passages. Daniel experienced God as a 'stream of flames' (Dan 7. 10) and, disturbed and alarmed by God's closeness, he fell on his face. Ezekiel also fell on his face and was struck dumb after his vision of God (Ezek 3. 24, 26). Closely related to these Old Testament events is the great vision of the apostles in the New Testament, known to us as the transfiguration of Christ (Mt 17. 1-6). The evangelist describes this vision as follows: 'Jesus took with him Peter and James and John his brother and led them up a high mountain apart. And he was transfigured before them, and his face shone like the sun, and his garments became white as light. And behold, there appeared to them Moses and Elijah, talking with him . . . When lo, a bright cloud overshadowed them and a voice from the cloud said, "This is my beloved son, with whom I am well pleased; listen to him". When the disciples heard this, they fell on their faces and were filled with awe'.

God's closeness, intensely experienced as in all these cases, always contains a threat. Man's whole being is deeply disturbed, even shattered. When we encounter God in this way, we receive a fulness of experience, but we are also burnt in our innermost being. For my fifth example, I should like to quote from the experience of Christ described in the secret revelation of the evangelist John, who reduced this experience to its barest essentials in the book of Revelation (Rev 1. 12-17): 'I turned to see the voice that was speaking to me and on turning I saw . . . one like a son of man . . . His head and his hair were white as white wool, white as snow; his eyes were like flames of fire, his feet were like burnished bronze, refined as in a furnace, as his voice was like the sound of many waters . . . and his face was like the sun shining in full strength. When I saw him, I fell at his feet as though dead'.

We should now be in a position to see a little more clearly what Jonah's flight from God really meant. Living close to God is not easy. When we pray at depth our whole existence is deeply disturbed. On the one hand, prayer may bring us the fulness of God's presence, but it is, on the other hand, also a way of suffering, painful struggle and abandonment. What, then, can we do? We must, I think, concentrate the whole of our prayer on Jesus Christ.

Christ saw God's glory during his life on this earth and did not hide his face. He received the deadly effect of this vision of God into his human nature and we can see the divine nature in a human form in his face. He

saw the Father unconcealed and this vision permeated
his whole existence. It no longer had a deadly effect. On
the contrary, God appeared to him as friendly and
attractive. He absorbed the disturbing, even shattering
effect of his encounter with God and was able to reveal
the Father to those whom he met. When Philip asked
him 'Show us the Father', he replied: 'He who has seen
me has seen the Father' (Jn 14. 9). In this, Christ has
provided us with a pattern for our prayer. Quietly,
discreetly and trustingly, we should touch his humanity
and through it sense the divine. It is this contact with
Jesus, this touching, that is important.

He was surrounded by a great crowd of people and
pushed about by them in Capharnaum. A poor woman
pressed through the crowd, reached Jesus and lightly
touched his garment. She was healed. 'Jesus said, "Who
was it that touched me?" When all denied it, Peter said,
"Lord, the multitudes surround you and press upon
you!" But Jesus said, "Someone touched me, for I
perceive that power has gone forth from me." And
when the woman saw that she was not hidden, she came
trembling, and falling down before him declared in the
presence of all the people why she had touched him and
how she had been immediately healed. And he said to
her, "Daughter, your faith has made you well. Go in
peace." ' (Luke 8. 45-48). The discreet, trusting gesture
of the sick woman of Capharnaum is the best attitude
for all of us when we pray.

The prophet's sleeping
The second image used in the book of Jonah to express
man's distance from God is Jonah's sleeping during the
storm at sea. There is something quite right in God's
letting us sleep. It is remarkable how often he lets us
doze off in the middle of the most real experiences. It is
as if he wanted us to know that they were not real.

How unreal our relationship with God is. We experience God's presence and are deeply disturbed by it.

Then we return to everyday life and are ashamed of ourselves for having had such frivolous thoughts. This is one of the greatest temptations of all. Our life with God is fragile and alien to our life in this world. We live with God, it is true to say, as though we were sleeping. We experience him in a mixture of certainty and inner doubt. We have to fight every day to regain that security. We are clearly not yet fully subject to God's power.

Romano Guardini has written with great understanding about this question in his book *The Lord*. Who really has power over me? he asks and then looks for an answer to this question. Those who speak to me, he replies. Those whose words I read. Those with whom I associate and even those who keep away from me. Those who give themselves to me and those who refuse to give themselves. Those who help me and those who obstruct me. Those who inhibit me. Those I care for and those I influence. These have power over me.

God, on the other hand, Guardini goes on, can only have power over me in spite of people. To the extent that I have time for God after people have made their demands on me. To the extent that I can still give my attention to him after their claims on me. To the extent that they do not influence me so much that I begin to think that he is not there. God can have power over me as long as my awareness of him can prevail over the demands and influence of my fellow men. His power can only be felt in spite of, through and together with them.

Guardini now turns from his fellow men and God to 'things' and God. Things, he declares, also have power over me. And he asks, what are these things that have such power? He gives several answers to this question. The things I want, through the power of my desire for them. The things that stand in my way, because they are an obstacle to me. The things that I encounter everywhere and at all times, because they stimulate me and claim my attention. And then he sums up. Things in themselves, all things have power over me, simply by being there and filling the world, my world, both within and without.

Things ... and God. Things have power over me, Guardini states, not God. God can only prevail in my life if there is a little room left for him among all these things. His power can only be felt in between them, outside them. But really, Guardini concludes sadly, he has no power over me. Every tree that stands in my path seems to have more power than he has, if only because it forces me to walk round it.

Finally, Guardini comes to God himself and his relationship with me. How would my life be if God really prevailed in it, he asks now. I would know — not by a slow, painful process of making him present in my thoughts, but in a constant, personal encounter with the living God — that he is real. I would know that he is God. That he is above all human concepts and names. I would know this as I know what I mean when I speak about a meadow full of lush vegetation and freshness that I have seen. I would know this as I am able to know another person, intimately, his shape, his way of walking, his habits, his attitudes.

If he really had power over me, God would be the point of departure, the way and the destiny of all my thoughts. His power would arouse my conscience and, transcending pure conscience, my power to love. I would, through his power in me, learn that the end of my life is a state of love existing between him and me. The kingdom of God would prevail in me.

But in our present situation, we have the kingdom of man, the kingdom of things, the kingdom of the powers and events of this world. They conceal God. They drive him out of our lives, to such an extent that he can only express himself in our lives on the fringe and in the intervals.

Who can really understand this, Guardini asks — that God is, that he is who he is and that everything that is exists only through him and would pass away like a

shadow if he withdrew his power? Do I really understand
that I am simply the work of his hands, his image and
likeness? Do I know that I know nothing of him? How
can that be? How can it be that a tree standing in my
path can be more real than God? How is it possible that
he should continue to be no more than a word? How is
it that he does not express his great power and penetrate
into the depths of my heart and mind?

Christ proclaimed the coming of the kingdom of God,
and in his preaching it is clearly something that is very
close. The kingdom of God can, however, only become
a reality if we are open to Christ's message. I think that
it is possible that, if Christ's message had met with a
positive response in faith in Israel, the kingdom of God
would indeed have come and we would now perhaps be
living in the situation which Guardini describes. The
rejection of Jesus and his message, however, resulted in
what may be called a 'second fall of man' and the
impossibility of bringing about the kingdom of God in
its originally planned form. The people did not believe
and did not change their way of living and thinking,
with the result that the kingdom of God did not come,
at least in the way in which it was first offered to man.

It remained as it were in suspense and is still in the
process of coming. It is present or almost present in
individuals and even in small groups of people, but
usually only for a short time. Then it fades from sight
again. A substitute was found by Jesus when he established the Church, which is, as it were, a bridge leading
to the kingdom of God that will only be realized at the
end of time. The Church is an interweaving of what is
already present with what does not yet exist. The
kingdom of God, the community of God and man that
will exist at the end of time, has already broken through
in the Church, but is not yet fully present. Every day we
have to begin again our task of establishing it. This is the
world in which Jonah was able to sleep in God's presence.
We too can simply go past God like sleep-walkers.

The sailors' distress caused by Jonah

Let us now examine the third image, that of the crew's distress caused by Jonah, and try to discover the essential message that it contains for us. So far, we have talked mainly about the objective fact of God's distance from us. We must now consider how we ourselves cause that distance from God. In other words, we must think about our own sins. Not about sin in general, but about our own completely personal rejection of God.

Most of us have at some time or other woken up in the morning, looked at ourselves in the mirror and quickly turned our face away. We had a glimpse of a strange, unknown face in the mirror and thought: who is that? At that moment, we ceased to make excuses or to speak in euphemisms. We were suddenly ourselves. At that moment, what we have done in life, what we possess, our skills and talents were all of no account. We stood there, unprotected, and were confronted by the ultimate question of man's existence: Who am I?

When we are faced with the task of reflecting about our own sins, we should certainly not try to call to mind every sin that we believe we have committed in the past. It is enough to consider only one sin — the sin of our life. This may not even be a very serious sin. But there is undoubtedly one sin in the life of each one of us that is central — an attitude, often revealed in certain habitual actions, which points clearly to our fallen nature. Each one of us has the task of discovering that sin. No one can help us in that search. It is only possible to give guidance. I would like to give just three indications here.

Firstly, if we were to look carefully, most of us would probably find selfishness somewhere beneath all our various sins. What, then, is my particular form of selfishness? I am not thinking here of the cruder forms of egotism which make men stop at nothing, even ruthless destructiveness, to gain their own ends. What I have in mind is more difficult to define. We are invariably inclined to refer everything that we do back to ourselves, so that it reflects our own glory. This basic need for self-glorification is rooted in our whole being and it is not often that we can eliminate it, even for a very short time. Even when we are behaving apparently quite selflessly, we still remain enslaved to this need to be admired. It is disturbing to see how many of the saints have, on their own admission, fought against this subtle form of selfishness and have still continued to be subject to it.

Secondly, who among us is really able to love? We all suffer, in one way or another, from a fundamental inability to love. Again and again, we betray those whom we most care for. There are times when we reach the summit of love. This may happen perhaps once in a lifetime. And then we spend the rest of our life taking back everything that we have given away during that period of brave, generous love. If we are to learn how to love only a little in the full sense of the word, we have to use all our strength to climb the steep slope of our own incapacity to love. Loving is basically giving ourselves totally to and living entirely from the other. To do this is to expose ourselves to uncertainty. Indeed our own life will be threatened. Love, then, is receiving our very being from the other — who is as unable to love as we are.

Thirdly, if we honestly examine our own incapacity for love, we shall undoubtedly discover that an inherent reluctance underlies all our actions. Love is basically saying Yes to the other's existence. Reluctance is saying No to his being and to everything that forms part of his life. Love says: The world has meaning for me only in you and through you. Without you, the world would be intolerable. Reluctance says: The whole world is meaningless to me as long as you are in it. With you, the world is intolerable. We may have repressed our reluctance, so that it expresses itself in strange forms — nervousness, antipathy, indifference and so on. Our loving is often full of reluctance. A superficial love

relationship often conceals a stronger force than reluctance — a will to destroy.

Let us now try to see where these three directions in
which our sin is perhaps moving converge and we shall
probably find the sin itself at that point. It is at first
difficult to recognize ourselves in the above description.
Surely we are not capable of that! Much more than our
own wickedness, however, is contained in this resistance
to God. It is paradoxical, but perhaps true to say that
we are worse than we really are. Our own individual
fallen state is simply an expression of the universally
fallen state of man.

Man's sinfulness is certainly a terrible mystery, but
we can always discover in all the sinfulness around us
something that belongs to our own existence. It is not
unfamiliar and completely outside ourselves, but familiar
to us and within ourselves. The sin of other people, the
sin of the community, the sin of mankind — that sin is
our sin. We are always intimately bound to our fellow-
men. We exist only in so far as we co-exist with other
people. The sin of the whole of mankind is present in
each one of our sins. The converse is also true — our
individual sin enters into all the sins of mankind.

As soon as we become aware of our sin, we at the
same time recognize that a need to resist God and to
revolt against his presence is deeply rooted in our
existence as men. At the beginning of the world, pure
spirits (legions of pure spirits) revolted against God. But
the essential characteristic of the spirit is to long with
every fibre of its being for God — it is driven with all its
existence towards God. If, then, resistance to God
occurs in such a spirit, its being driven irresistibly
towards God is surely converted into a radical resistance,
culminating in revolt.

What, then is expressed in human sin is the resistance
of the pure spirits or angels. The sin of the angels is the
model for our existence as creatures and we are therefore
predisposed to resist God. In all the little sins that we

commit, often unseen, every day, we are trying to imitate
the angels in their revolt against God. There are therefore
different levels of human sin, although these sometimes
overlap and they are always open to each other. We may
say that there is our personal sin and, within and behind
this, the sins of mankind and, within and behind these,
the sin of the spirits.

All this is, of course, quite terrible and terrifying. But
there is, on the other hand, something comforting in it,
because, if we are ever able to overcome in ourselves
even the smallest sin, we shall have done something of
universal signficance. We shall have blocked the source
of evil, not only in ourselves, but also in the whole of
mankind, in the world and even in the cosmos. Our
action will have helped to save the world.

If we understand this properly, we shall have understood the meaning of penance. It is true, of course, that
we poison the whole of mankind with our sin and that
we are also poisoned by the sin of the whole of mankind.
But this sin is counterbalanced by penance, which shares
in the redemption of the world.

A prayer

Jesus once told this story: 'There was a man who had two sons; and the younger one of them said to the father, "Father, give me the share of property that falls to me". And he divided his living between them. Not many days later, the younger son gathered all he had and took his journey into a far country and there he squandered his property in loose living. And when he had spent everything, a great famine arose in that country and he began to be in want. So he went and joined himself to one of the citizens of that country, who sent him into the fields to feed swine. And he would gladly have fed on the pods that the swine ate, but no one gave him anything. But when he came to himself, he said, "How many of my father's hired servants have bread enough and to spare, but I perish here with hunger! I will arise and go to my father and I will say to him, 'Father, I have sinned against heaven and before you; I am no longer worthy to be called your son; treat me as one of your hired servants' ". And he arose and came to his father. But while he was still at a distance, his father saw him and had compassion and ran and embraced him and kissed him. And the son said to him, "Father, I have sinned against heaven and before you; I am no longer worthy to be called your son". But the father said to the servants, "Bring quickly the best robe and put it on him; and put a ring on his hand and shoes on his feet; and bring the fatted calf and kill it and let us eat and make merry; for this my son was dead and is alive again; he was lost and is found". And they began to make merry' (Luke 15. 11-24).

Lord, our father, we ask you to let us understand you and your great mercy and to make it possible for us to encounter our brothers and sisters in the same understanding. Amen.

Redemption in descent

Our lives are always situated somewhere between closeness to God and distance from God. This is the provisional result of our meditations. Towards the end, we were beginning to sense something of God's mercy. We can begin our third meditation, then, precisely at that point. Two events in the life of the prophet Jonah may help to determine the direction in which our meditation should move. The first is Jonah's experience in the belly of the sea monster and the second is God's giving the task to Jonah a second time.

Going down
The sailors had thrown Jonah into the sea and the storm had ceased at once. The crew were safe and soon forgot the man they had thrown overboard. 'The Lord appointed a great fish to swallow up Jonah; and Jonah was in the belly of the fish three days and three nights' (Jon 1. 17).

This strange event assumes universal dimensions in the prophecy of Christ: 'Some of the scribes and pharisees said to him, "Teacher, we wish to see a sign from you". But he answered them, "An evil and adulterous generation seeks for a sign; but no sign shall be given except the sign of the prophet Jonah. For as Jonah was three days and three nights in the belly of the whale, so will the Son of man be three days and three nights in the heart of the earth" (Mt 12. 38-40).

This statement must be accepted in the form that Jesus made it: 'I will go down into the heart of the earth'. Jonah is seen here as prefiguring the Redeemer in his most decisive act of redemption — his going down into the heart of the earth, that is, into the innermost depths of reality. Later on, I should like to say something that I believe is very important about this going down, but for the present we can read Jonah's prayer and think of it as the prayer of Christ before he died:

'I called to the Lord out of my distress and he answered me; out of the belly of Sheol I cried, and thou didst hear my voice. For thou didst cast me into the deep, into the heart of the seas, and the flood was around me; all thy waves and thy billows passed over me. Then I said, "I am cast out from thy presence; how shall I again look upon thy holy temple?" The waters closed in over me, the deep was round about me; weeds wrapped about my head at the roots of the mountains. I went down to the land whose bars closed upon me for ever; yet thou didst bring up my life from the pit, O Lord my God' (2. 2-6).

This prayer expresses an essential element of our relationship with God, namely that we are saved by going down. The mystics called this experience 'night'. It is a situation in which we are apparently abandoned by everyone and everything and left a prey to tormenting doubts. If we are to understand what this 'night' really means, we call to mind the metaphysical meaning of 'light'. In the West, light has always been a symbol for knowledge, openness and translucence. 'Night' is the very opposite — a going down into a closed, opaque sphere where nothing can be known. Night is also distance from God.

All these meanings have to be borne in mind if we are to appreciate the significance of the statement that we are saved by going down. Correctly interpreted, this statement can show us clearly how it is possible for modern man to find his way back to God and recognize his dependence on God in and through his experience of being unfulfilled, exposed and abandoned.

In this context, I would like to quote a passage by

Georg Trakl on revelation and going down. Despite the symbolism which it contains and which is admittedly difficult to interpret, I think that it expresses this situation perfectly: 'Journey without peace through wild rocks far from the evening hamlets, homecoming shepherds; far off the sinking sun grazes on crystal meadow and its wild singing, the lonely call of the bird vibrates, fading away in blue tranquillity. But gently you come in the night, as I lay awake on the hill or raging in the spring storm. And blacker and blacker melancholy clouds the separated head, shuddering flashes of lightning terrify the nocturnal soul, your hands tear my breathless breast'.

There is a practice in English Jesuit houses of reading the 'menology' every evening. This consists of short descriptions of the lives of holy or famous Jesuit fathers. I heard this menology for a whole year and quite honestly I have forgotten it all, with the exception of one description, that of an unknown lay brother. It was not even an account of the man's life, but just a letter written by him.

During the sixteenth century, this man was sent by his superiors from England to Rome. On the voyage he was taken prisoner by Turkish pirates and sold as a slave. For many years he was an oarsman, a galley slave. One day, he found that he could send a letter and this eventually reached his home land. Since then, this letter has been read aloud once a year, on the day that it arrived in England. Without self-pity, this lay brother-galley slave describes the conditions of his life and his own attitude. Although he has had several opportunities to escape, he says, he has decided not to take them. Far from his brothers in religion, without the comfort either of religion or his fellow men and exposed to great suffering, he has, he says, finally found Christ. He calls himself Christ's slave. For the first time in his life he is truly happy. Apart from this letter, nothing is known about this lay brother.

It is good for us to know that such people as this have lived and still live, because they reveal to us the real foundations of faith. So many of us today are caught up in the treadmill of everyday living, have no time to meditate and are in constant danger of becoming totally superficial in our attitude. It is therefore a great comfort to know that there are such slaves of Christ who have completely accepted their suffering and have in this way penetrated to the heart of God himself. They do more than simply enter themselves into the heart of God — they also take us and the whole of Christendom into that heart. They are precursors of eternity and heralds of glory.

Another Jesuit whose suffering has often moved me deeply is Jean-Joseph Surin. This mystic was born in 1600 in Bordeaux. He died in the same town sixty-five years later. We know very little about the first thirteen years of his life. When he was thirteen, however, he encountered Christ in a mystical experience for the first time. He was at vespers in the chapel of the Carmelite nuns when Christ came tangibly close to him and gave him the certainty of being specially chosen. He joined the Society of Jesus in 1615.

In 1630 he began his active work. He became a spiritual director and it was not long before he was recognized as one of the most gifted — and this in a century noted for its spirituality. His fame spread rapidly and this was helped by his letters, which were copied, distributed widely and read everywhere, even in the most select circles. It became fashionable to possess originals or at least copies of these letters.

At about that time, a very strange phenomenon was taking place in the town of Loudun in the diocese of Poitiers. An entire community of Ursuline nuns was possessed by the devil. It was widely assumed that the parish priest, Urbain Grandier, had laid a spell on the nuns. He was arrested and quickly put to death, but the convent continued to be possessed by the devil. Someone, however, remembered the well-known spiritual director Surin, who came to Loudun, stayed a few months and helped to improve the situation a little.

Nothing was fundamentally changed, however, and on 28 November 1637, during morning prayers, Surin offered up his life for the sisters. He put his life at the disposal of the devil, who was to take possession of it and leave the nuns in peace. The next day, the inhabitants of the town were struck by the unusual peace in the convent, went there and were received by perfectly healthy sisters. A solitary figure left the convent in a state of spiritual darkness, perhaps mentally disturbed. It was Jean-Joseph Surin.

He spent the rest of his life in Bordeaux. Gradually he lost his power of speech and in the end became completely dumb. He also became blind and deaf. Now and then, apparently seized by superhuman strength, he would scream aloud, roll on the floor and try to throw himself out of the window. Twice he succeeded and was found with broken limbs. He thought that he was damaged for ever and cursed God. At the same time, however, he often knelt for hours in front of the tabernacle without saying a word. Frequently he regained his reason for minutes or even hours on end and wrote remarkable poems about the mystery of God and later little books on the spiritual life.

For the last three years of his life, he was quite normal. He wrote a series of books summarizing his twenty-five years of suffering. It is disturbing to read the letters that he wrote after his long period of spiritual darkness, resuming the dialogue at precisely the point where it had been broken off a quarter of a century before, just as though nothing had happened in the meantime. His letter to Abbé de Vaut, for instance, begins with the words: 'Circumstances have prevented me from replying to you at once. Please forgive me. The Lord recently gave me all my senses back and I am making use of them at once to write to you'. He died on Good Friday, 21 April 1665, after having asked the whole community to forgive him.

No one can predict how God will act with us. It is, of course, possible to object that Jean-Joseph Surin's life was quite out of the ordinary and that it would not be too difficult to find explanations for it. Very often, however, it will be said that his life could be taken as a model for holiness. This may well be true. What, however, cannot be disputed is that two processes are intimately connected in the soul of man — suffering and maturity. The soul's ascent to God often takes place in the inner room of suffering.

Saint John of the Cross has written with great insight about this. God, he said, spreads his night over the intellect and paralyzes the will. The memory becomes empty and the heart heavy with melancholy. In the depth of his soul, however, man remains united with God. There, an inexpressible light shines in the middle of the night. Yet even that makes the soul despair, because it cannot understand how it can receive this light when it is so given over to darkness. The soul is therefore seized with heavy suffering, to such an extent that death would come as salvation. This, John of the Cross assures us, happens to every man who comes close to God.

In this mysterious interplay between darkness and light, we can sense the meaning of suffering — its meaning, but not its justification. Suffering cannot have any justification. We cannot explain it or find any reason for it. All that we can do is to remain open to the mystery of human suffering and sense its meaning within that mystery. A free world is always a world that may suffer. But we can only reach God if we are free. Is that an answer or a justification? No, we are always able to refuse, resist or rebel. We must learn to see this clearly and understand it fully. It is always possible for us to rebel, but in this is revealed a mystery that silences our questioning. This silence in the presence of suffering is an essential aspect of Christian prayer. Let me conclude, then, by saying that the heart of Christian prayer is the prayer of Gethsemane.

Christ's descent into hell

It would be quite wrong, even impossible, to speak about going down and redemption and not to mention the mystery of Christ's going down into hell. It is certainly surprising how few sermons are based on this theme and how terribly superficial most of those few sermons are.

The first question that we have to consider in this context is the term itself: descent into hell. At the very least it is misleading. Christ himself was much more precise when he spoke about his going down into the heart of the earth. By this, of course, he meant that he let himself be swallowed up, in his death, into the innermost centre of the earth. Today, this is no more than a rather vivid image. At the time when the words were spoken, however, it was a reality, since men had a metaphysical conception of geography. For men with a geocentric view of the world, then, the centre of the earth meant the middle of the universe. It meant this, moreover, not simply in the geographical sense, but in the metaphysical sense. Christ went down, in other words, into the physical, geographical centre of the earth, but at the same time he entered the essential being of all things and the inner, central reality of the whole of history. The heart of the earth is the point where everything lives in a state of interpenetration.

The heart of the earth. It is certainly easier to grasp what is meant by this going down if we think of it as a going down into the heart, as Christ himself described it. The word is entirely human and primordial. The heart of man is the very centre of his being, in which he grows, evolves and is contained as a concrete, personal unity. When we speak of the heart of man, we mean, in a word, what he is. Similarly, when we speak of the heart of the earth, we are immediately aware of the central essence from which the world develops, the unity in which it is rooted.

Christ emptied himself, died and went down into the

heart of the earth. In doing this, he gave himself utterly to the whole world and the whole of history. He also gave himself to each one of us individually. This very movement down into the unity in which the world is rooted, this sinking of his entire divine life into essential being of the world, was at the same time his resurrection.

Christ, we may say, is in the midst and the middle of the misery of our earth, the world to which we are so indissolubly bound. He is here, among us, as the mysterious law and the innermost being of all things. I should like to discuss one or two aspects of this mystery later on, but for the time being let me simply say that our world has been sanctified and redeemed by Christ's descent into hell and show briefly how this has come about.

Christ's mercy
One aspect of this question of redemption in going down ought to be mentioned at once. It is this. Contrary to all our expectations, there is evidence that our suffering has a positive value. In the depth of our being there is always a conviction, which cannot be accounted for simply rationally, that hope can only reveal what it really is when our existence is threatened.

We should question ourselves very seriously and as profoundly as possible: Is it possible or desirable to be without suffering, danger or threat in our lives? Would our lives perhaps not be shallow or empty without them? They are, after all, the other side of the coin known as grace. They are not grace in themselves, but the Lord has made them into grace. The Lord has sanctified our suffering and from being a reality that is always with us it has become a way to him.

I see before me the whole world immersed in God's mercy. Mercy exists all around us, not an anonymous mercy, but the mercy of Christ. Christ revealed this mercy to us in his life on earth. The whole gospel of Luke contains this revelation and it is worth reading it from this point of view alone. A shorter account of the revelation of Christ's mercy can be found in the story of the resurrection of Lazarus. If we meditate about these descriptions of God's mercy as revealed in Christ, what we experience is a second encounter. I have met this person before. I have experienced his mercy before in my life. When we encounter Christ in this way, we know that we have already met him, that we have always known him and we become suddenly aware of the part that he has always played in our lives.

God is always making a new beginning

Finally God caught up with Jonah who was running away from him: 'The Lord spoke to the fish and it vomited out Jonah upon the dry land. Then the word of the Lord came to Jonah the second time, saying, "Arise, go to Nineveh, that great city, and proclaim to it the message that I tell you". So Jonah arose and went to Nineveh, according to the word of the Lord' (2. 10 - 3. 3).

We could almost say here that everything was beginning all over again in Jonah's life. And it would be true to say that. God is not discouraged by our lack of faithfulness. We turn away from him, but his grace continues and even increases. We cannot and should not measure the extent of his grace according to the limits of our own heart. His heart is always greater than our human heart.

The source of our trust — and our disquiet — is that God is always making a new beginning. There are no closed books, no finished businesses in the life of a Christian. There is no safeguard against God. We cannot tie his hands. We cannot keep him out by our sins and faithlessness and we cannot even keep him out by our devotions and prayers. One of the basic facts of Christian life is that God is always making a new beginning.

When he makes a new beginning with us, he always holds on to us. Despite all the pious — and often superficial — protests to the contrary, his plans can often be frustrated. In his interventions into human history, he has to deal with man's freedom and this endangers his plans. Yet, despite man's disobedience and rebellion, God remains faithful. Whenever man frustrates his plan of salvation, he makes the cause of frustration itself the point of departure for a new way to grace.

God's will and his activity are unchanging. His love is unchanging. It will not be halted, deflected or repelled. It can transform everything, even repulsion, into an even greater movement of love. God's way of acting is to make everything into a new beginning. It is not absurd to say of him that everything goes with him from beginnings to beginnings through beginnings and on to the final beginning.

God's excessiveness

This law can be recognized most easily if we consider it in the light of the history of man's salvation. It may help if I give a very short outline here of the main stages in that history. At each important stage in the history of our salvation, God makes a new beginning with man and this law, which I shall call the law of God's excessiveness, is revealed.

In the beginning, God made his plans known to man. Man was to live in direct contact with God, close to him, directly in him, in a world in which everything that existed and everything that happened was also directly in God, known in him, loved in him and received from him.

The first man and woman, however, lost this precious gift for ever. We must not lose ourselves here in speculation, asking ourselves why and how this came about. We must simply accept, for the purpose of our meditation, that the first man and woman delivered the whole of mankind, all of us, up to suffering and death. God, however, was not defeated. He at once made a new beginning. He made a new plan for man and the world, with new laws and new ways to him. From the fallen state of man and the world, God created a new state of salvation. He began again at a new level and in a new direction.

Mankind increased and multiplied, but man's instincts, stemming from the savage nature that he had brought with him from the animal kingdom, gained the upper hand and he soon began once more to show signs of decadence or, to use a simpler word with the same basic meaning, signs of fall. The song of Lamech expresses this fallen nature in a terrifying way: 'Adah and Zillah, hear my voice; you wives of Lamech, hearken to what I say: I have slain a man for wounding me, a young man for striking me. If Cain is avenged sevenfold, truly Lamech seventy-sevenfold' (Gen 4. 23-24). Surely God could do no more with this race of men. But he did not give up. He chose a little group of people, saved them and let the rest of mankind go down in the flood. With the little remnant he made a new beginning.

Noah's salvation marked a new beginning, but the goal had not yet been reached. Mankind was in great confusion at Babel, and God scattered the inhabitants over the whole earth. Once again he had to make a new beginning. He took a handful of people from the great mass of mankind and began again with Abraham and his family.

A small nomadic clan descended from Abraham's line. These nomads were driven by hunger to Egypt. They were able to live there in relative security, but gradually they forgot their vocation. God took action. He drove them out of the comfort and safety of Egypt into the desert and let a whole generation of them die there. With the few who survived, the little remnant, those who had been born in the desert and had experienced his power there, God made another new beginning.

God wanted above all to be the leader of this people in everything. He wanted above all to redeem them in dialogue with the whole people. But they wanted political security. They wanted institutions. And that, in those days, meant a king. God allowed them to defect in this way. He permitted his plan to become secularized. Then, much later, the political safety of the people was once again destroyed when they were taken captive and led into exile in Babylonia.

But even in captivity they experienced God's new beginning with them. With the little remnant of Israelites who had remained true to him, he established an inner kingdom. Captivity produced men whose image of God was pure and spiritual and who fervently awaited the coming of the Messiah. God's law was central in their lives. God's plan was to build a messianic kingdom among this little remnant.

Even in the heart of this faithfulness to God's law, there was a new falling away. Men's expectation of the Messiah gradually became externalized and institutionalized. When Jesus came and proclaimed the immanent kingdom of God, he was rejected by the very remnant of Jews who had been preparing for his coming. God's new beginning in Christ was frustrated. But Christ himself transformed God's plan by postponing the coming of the kingdom until the end of time and choosing for himself the way of suffering. Jesus' transformation of God's series of new beginnings with man was the death on the cross.

God did not give way to man's attempts to frustrate his plan. Once again he chose a remnant and founded his Church on these men. To make this beginning definitive, Christ chose death and became a risen body. In other words, he made it possible for us to grow together with his pneumatic, spiritual body. In this way, he made a definitive breakthrough by means of which we can continue to grow and mature on the way to glory.

God's new beginning in our lives

The same history of salvation takes place every day in the life of each one of us. Let me conclude this outline that I began in the previous section with a sad, but at the same time comforting story. Some three hundred years ago, the Jesuit missionaries and many of their converts in Japan suffered terrible persecution. The Christians fled to remote villages in an attempt to escape, but the emperor's soldiers found them and they were forced either to renounce their faith or to die. Many did give up the Christian religion in order to avoid torture and death. Others were killed quite quickly. Some died only after long and painful torture. However they died, they are now honoured as martyrs.

At that time, a young Jesuit, Christopher Ferreira, a man who was clearly a born leader, was living in Europe. His superiors decided to send him to Japan with the task of animating the missionary work there, organizing resistance, comforting the persecuted and above all encouraging them to persist in faith.

Ferreira went to Japan disguised as a merchant and was not molested when he entered the country. He set to work without delay and was soon active in the Christian communities, inspiring them with courage and hope. An underground organization was created, enabling Christians to meet without attracting too much attention, console each other and celebrate the Eucharist together. Ferreira was regarded as the saviour of the Japanese mission.

On 18 October 1633, the imperial police arrested him and many other Christians during a celebration of Mass. On that day no one wanted to renounce his faith and the torture and the killing began. Everyone who was arrested during Mass on that day stood firm — everyone except the man who had been sent to Japan to encourage the others to persist in faith. Only Christopher Ferreira denied that he was a Christian.

But that was not all. Because he had not been steadfast, hundreds of others denied their faith. In court, there were many who were condemned for their faith, but also very many who were released when they retracted.

For Ferreira it was not enough to have bought his life for the price of his faith — he also served as interpreter in the trials. A leading Jesuit had become a leading apostate, calling on his brothers and sisters in Christ to repudiate their faith.

This story does not end here. Nineteen years later, in 1653, Ferreira, who was now an old man of seventy-four, stood up during a trial and spoke. We do not know precisely what he said, but his words must have been more or less: 'I can bear it no longer. I would rather die. Kill me as well. I am a Christian'.

He was seized at once and tortured. This time, however, he remained steadfast and in the end died as a martyr. The old man achieved what the young man failed to do. His name is now among the list of the hundred and eleven Japanese martyrs of the Society of Jesus.

This story can therefore be a source of comfort to us. Whatever happens to us, whatever we may do against God and our fellow men, whatever we may have done and may do in the future, and even if we do what Christopher Ferreira did — it is never too late. God is always making a new beginning. In the life of every Christian, the world always begins again at that moment.

The tenderness of God

We come now to the final episodes in the life of the prophet Jonah. I have to admit that this last meditation has presented me with great difficulties. The end of this most unusual story is so rich in insights that it is not at all easy to confine oneself to a few points.

God is unaccountable
We can, however, begin by saying something about Jonah's annoyance. He had preached God's word in Nineveh and had prophesied that the city would be destroyed within forty days. Then the inhabitants of the city had done what Jonah himself was unable or unwilling to do — they had changed their ways and become converted: 'When God saw what they did, how they turned from their evil way, God repented of the evil which he had said he would do to them; and he did not do it' (3. 10).

We must try to put ourselves into Jonah's situation. Everything pointed to the fact that he was a false prophet who had upset God's plan. 'This displeased Jonah exceedingly and he was angry. And he prayed to the Lord and said, "I pray thee, Lord, is not this what I said when I was yet in my country? This is why I made haste to flee to Tarshish; for I knew that thou art a gracious God and merciful, slow to anger and abounding in steadfast love, and repentest of evil. Therefore now, O Lord, take my life from me, I beseech thee, for it is better for me to die than to live' (4. 1-3).

What emerges from this unexpected turn in the story is that God is above all unaccountable. We have to renounce ourselves completely if we are to enter into a relationship with him. We have to accept that he is beyond our understanding. It is said of Gautama Buddha that, when he was a young prince, he once stood up and simply walked out of his palace into homelessness. We too can and must give up our familiar, safe environment and give ourselves wholly to God who is impossible to understand.

It would not be difficult for a Jesuit to find evidence of this experience in the history of his own order. There has been a dialectical tension in the Society of Jesus ever since it was first founded for the purpose of defending Catholic teaching and missionizing the non-Christian world. Its rapid and successful advance strengthened this inner contradiction and the very people who had first promoted its establishment rejected it and condemned its positive commitment.

This tension has not only been revealed in individual incidents of lesser importance. It has always been present in the history of the order's commitment to the greater glory of God and the future of the Church. We must, however, give an example of this and perhaps the most striking is the great controversy that began about three or four hundred years ago in China and Europe around the person of Matteo Ricci.

Ricci had evolved a radically new missionary method by adapting Christianity to Chinese ideas. He made use of everything in Chinese culture that could in one way or another be reconciled to Christian teaching and proclaimed Christian truth to the Chinese people with the help of their own wisdom and philosophical concepts. The scholastic method that was so favoured in the Europe of his time was quietly dropped. Even the pope encouraged him. He was also allowed to create a distinctively Chinese rite. This was so effective that he was able to gain access to the Chinese court and the conversion of the whole of China was within sight.

It was then that he was attacked by many theologians

who had never been in China. These men were convinced
that Christian teaching and western culture were indissolubly united. To give up the western form of expressing
faith was to give up faith itself. The pope removed his
support for Ricci's venture and condemned his missionary
work. Today we see the result — the conversion of China
is less advanced today than it was when Ricci was active
there.

It is true, of course, that in our own century Pope
Pius XII declared that Ricci's method was the best, the
only possible method for converting non-European
people to the Christian faith. But it was too late. Why, we
are bound to ask, did this have to happen? Why do such
things still happen? Perhaps God will give us the answer
to this question at the last judgment. In the meantime,
we must accept the mystery and recognize that God often
seems to 'attack' us unexpectedly in our own lives.

God's humour

We have considered how unaccountable God is in his
dealings with man. Let us now turn to another aspect of
God's nature — one that is certainly very often neglected
in our thinking about him. Whereas Jonah was quite
lacking in humour, God possessed — and possesses — it
to an infinite degree.

The exegetes may not agree with my interpretation,
but I cannot help thinking of the episode of the castor-oil
plant as God's practical joke: 'The Lord God appointed
a castor-oil plant and made it come up over Jonah, that
it might be a shade over his head, to save him from his
discomfort. So Jonah was exceedingly glad because of
the castor-oil plant. But when dawn came up the next
day, God appointed a worm which attacked the plant,
so that it withered. When the sun arose, God appointed
a sultry east wind, and the sun beat upon the head of
Jonah so that he was faint; and he asked that he might
die, and said, "It is better for me to die than to live" '
(4. 6-8).

I am sure that God is performing a practical joke here.
If we are entirely humourless through our own fault, we
may be sinning. A man is humourless when he can no
longer laugh at himself. What is humour? A great deal
that people call humour has nothing really to do with
humour at all. Humour is not just being funny. It is not
a thoughtless gaiety. It is never superficial. It is never
frivolous.

What is humour, then? It is always deep and reflective.
It is cheerful, but with what Dante called *la grande
tristezza*, a deep sadness. It is a cheerful seriousness. It is
serious because it hides a fundamental wisdom that
recognizes that nothing human is ever perfect. At the
same time, however, it is filled with the complete
certainty that everything is good because everything is
subject to God's grace.

A philosopher once said: 'Humour is when we laugh
in spite of everything'. Cervantes quoted Don Quixote,
the man who was folly itself, as man himself. His hero is
full of humour and arouses humour because his folly is
loveable. His humour is conscious of need, suffering and
evil in the world. At the same time, however, it knows
that these are not the ultimate values in life.

The man who has humour in his soul also has the will
to live. He can live without illusions. He can also say Yes
to life with complete certainty. Humour is critical, but
it is capable of reconciling. It is patient and endlessly
tolerant. It lets everything that is exist simply because it
is there and forms part of man's environment. It is
critical, yes, but it always criticizes itself first. But let us
draw the inevitable conclusion from all this — to take
oneself too seriously and not to be able to laugh about
oneself is a sign of deep irreligiosity.

The inner essence of humour is to be found in the
power of man's religiousness. Humour sees man as quite
inadequate in the presence of God. It also sees him,
however, in the mirror of God's love, even though there
is no need to speak about God. Humour expresses itself

with resignation, in the knowledge that man and all that surrounds him is imperfect. But this resignation is also overcome in the certainty that everything finite is enclosed within God's infinite grace. Humour is therefore a love of the world, especially when that world reveals its folly and its inadequacy. The man who possesses humour loves the world, not only in spite of its imperfection, but also and above all because of its imperfection. Love, after all, says Yes to everything that exists and experiences genuine happiness because it exists. The love of the world experienced by humour, then, is also a happiness because of the world. Humour thanks God that it can live in such an imperfect world.

All deeply religious men have been full of humour. They understand everything, forgive everything and above all they do not take everything seriously. I might go so far as to say — we should not always take God so very seriously. He, after all, is capable of joking. Why should God be humourless? He sees into our hearts and surrounds the whole world with his mercy. That is why I am convinced that humour must have a place in our relationship with God.

Abraham, our father in faith, is also our example here. We read in the Bible how Abraham laughed: 'God said to Abraham, "As for Sarai your wife . . . I will bless her and I will give you a son by her. I will bless her and she shall be a mother of nations; kings and peoples shall come from her". Then Abraham fell on his face and laughed, and said to himself, "Shall a child be born to a man who is a hundred years old?" ' (Gen 17. 15-17).

God stood in front of Abraham and we have seen how terrifying God's presence can be. Yet this man laughs in God's presence. He really laughed — fell down on his face and could not stop laughing. He really believed that God was able to perform this miracle, but he felt that it was funny enough to laugh about.

I have said that Abraham was our father in faith. We should remember that in this episode. He fell on his face

twice. The first time because of God's infinite glory.
The second time — here — because he was laughing.
These two belong together. The man who can fall down
in adoration can also fall down and laugh. Irenaeus, who
lived in the second century, once said: *Gloria Dei vivens
homo*. These almost untranslatable words mean, I think:
God is most glorified in a man who is full of life (and
the joy of living).

I have only given two indications for our spiritual life
from the final episodes in the book of Jonah. The first is
that man has to give up himself and learn to live in
uncertainty if he wants to be completely with God. The
second is that the really religious man must learn to
smile peacefully, understandingly and lovingly. All this,
however, is just said in passing so that I can say what I
do not want to say explicitly.

God's patience

At the end of the book of Jonah is a song of praise to
God's patience. It was tenderness — the mildness — of
God that drove Jonah to despair: 'I knew that thou art a
gracious and merciful God, slow to anger and abounding
in steadfast love and that thou repentest of evil' (4. 2).
After he had played the trick on Jonah with the castor-
oil plant, God taught him a lesson about his mildness.
'God said to Jonah, "Do you do well to be angry for the
plant?" And he said, "I do well to be angry, angry
enough to die". And the Lord said, "You pity the plant,
for which you did not labour, nor did you make it grow.
It came into being in a night and perished in a night.
And should I not pity Nineveh, that great city, in which
there are more than a hundred and twenty thousand
persons, who do not know their right hand from their
left, and also much cattle?" ' (4. 9-11).

God is tender. He thinks of children — they are the
ones who do not know the difference between right and
left — and animals. There is always a time of concealment, affecting not only the individual aspects of

Christian truth, but also that truth itself. Then the historical situation changes, often quite suddenly, and Christians have to look at the revelation of Christ from a different point of view and with different eyes. It is at times like these that they often discover that they have been neglecting an essential aspect of Christian truth, perhaps for a very long period. An example of this is slavery. Another is torture. Nowadays, no Christian would doubt for a moment that both these practices are entirely contradictory to fundamental Christian teaching. Yet this truth, obvious to us now, was not perceived by Christians in the past. An enormous change had to take place in the structure of society and in human thinking before Christians could recognize how unChristian slavery and torture were.

It would seem that the time of concealment has come to an end now as far as Christian mildness is concerned. We have become acutely aware of the truth of Christ's teaching about the need for us to reject violence and be completely defenceless and vulnerable in our dealings with each other. We have discovered the power of tenderness and we may, because of this, be standing at a turning-point in Christian history. There are Christians today who are as totally committed to the practice of mildness as Christians in the early Church were committed to martyrdom. Let me quote a number of texts from the New Testament which have a bearing on this and may help to clarify the total demand that Christ makes on us.

Christ's demand
We read in the fifth chapter of Matthew's gospel: 'I tell you, unless your righteousness exceeds that of the scribes and pharisees, you will never enter the kingdom of heaven. You have heard that it was said to the men of old, "You shall not kill" and whoever kills shall be liable to judgment. But I say to you that everyone who is angry with his brother shall be liable to judgment; whoever insults his brother shall be liable to the council and

whoever says "You fool!" shall be liable to the hell of fire. So if you are offering your gift at the altar and there remember that your brother has something against you, leave your gift there before the altar and go; first be reconciled with your brother and then come and offer your gift . . . You have heard that it was said, "An eye for an eye and a tooth for a tooth". But I say to you, Do not resist one who is evil. But if any one strikes you on the right cheek, turn to him the other also; and if any one would sue you and take your coat, let him have your cloak as well; and if any one forces you to go one mile, go with him two miles. Give to him who begs from you and do not refuse him who would borrow from you. You have heard that it was said, "You shall love your neighbour and hate your enemy". But I say to you, Love your enemies and pray for those who persecute you, so that you may be sons of your Father who is in heaven; for he makes the sun rise on the evil and on the good and sends down rain on the just and the unjust. For if you love those who love you, what reward have you? Do not even the tax collectors do the same? And if you salute only your brethren, what more are you doing than others? Do not even the gentiles do the same? You, therefore, must be perfect, as your heavenly Father is perfect' (Mt 5. 20-24, 38-48).

In the sixth chapter of the gospel according to Luke, this train of thought is continued: 'I say to you that hear, Love your enemies, do good to those who hate you, bless those who curse you, pray for those who abuse you. To him who strikes you on the cheek, offer the other also; from him who takes away your cloak, do not withhold your coat as well. Give to every one who begs from you and of him who takes away your goods, do not ask for them again. If you love those who love you, what credit is that to you? For even sinners love those who love them . . . But love your enemies and do good. Lend, expecting nothing in return; and your reward will be great and you will be sons of the Most

High, for he is kind (mild) to the ungrateful and selfish.
Be merciful, even as your Father is merciful. Judge not,
and you will not be judged; condemn not, and you will
not be condemned; forgive, and you will be forgiven'
(Lk 6. 27-32, 35-37).

Let us now look at the beatitudes, which precede
these passages in both gospels. First, Luke's shorter
version: 'Blessed are you poor, for yours is the kingdom
of God. Blessed are you that weep now, for you shall
laugh. Blessed are you when men hate you, and when
they exclude you and revile you, and cast out your name
as evil, on account of the Son of Man!' (Lk 6. 20-22).

Then the longer version of Matthew. When we read
this, we should notice especially the sentences that are
not in Luke. I have marked these with an asterisk,
because they are particularly important for us: 'Blessed
are the poor in spirit, for theirs is the kingdom of heaven.
Blessed are those who mourn, for they shall be comforted.
Blessed are the meek, for they shall inherit the earth.*
Blessed are those who hunger and thirst for righteousness,
for they shall be satisfied. Blessed are the merciful, for
they shall obtain mercy.* Blessed are the pure in heart,
for they shall see God.* Blessed are the peacemakers,
for they shall be called sons of God.* Blessed are those
who are persecuted for righteousness' sake, for theirs is
the kingdom of heaven. Blessed are you when men revile
you and persecute you and utter all kinds of evil against
you falsely on my account' (Mt 5. 3-11).

Let us now meditate about the important passage in
Paul's letter to the Romans: 'Repay no one evil for evil,
but take thought for what is noble in the sight of all. If
possible, so far as it depends on you, live peaceably with
all. Beloved, never avenge yourselves ... No, if your
enemy is hungry, feed him; if he is thirsty, give him to
drink ... Do not be overcome by evil, but overcome evil
with good' (Rom 12. 17-21).

In the first letter to the Corinthians, Paul describes
Christian love: 'Love is patient and kind; love is not

jealous or boastful; it is not arrogant or rude. Love does
not insist on its own way; it is not irritable or resentful;
it does not rejoice at wrong, but rejoices in the right.
Love bears all things, believes all things, hopes all things,
endures all things' (1 Cor 13. 4-7).

The mildness of Christ is for us the way of redemption.
Paul has written about this too: 'We ourselves were once
foolish, disobedient, led astray, slaves to various passions
and pleasures, passing our days in malice and envy, hated
by men and hating one another; but when the goodness
and loving kindness of God our Saviour appeared, he
saved us . . . by renewal in the Holy Spirit' (Tit 3. 3-5).

The mildness of Christ is God breaking through,
powerfully but without violence, into our violent world.
Peter wanted to save him by the sword, but Jesus at
once said to him, 'Put your sword back into its place;
for all who take the sword will perish by the sword. Do
you think that I cannot appeal to my Father, and he
will at once send me more than twelve legions of angels?'
(Mt 26. 52-53).

God, who holds the whole of creation in his hands
and whose power is limitless, never resorts to violence.
Only those who are really strong can be really tender.
Jesus was saying very much the same as this when he
spoke to Pilate: 'My kingship is not of this world. If my
kingship were of this world, my servants would fight, so
that I might not be handed over to the Jews. But my
kingship is not of this world' (Jn 18. 36).

We could give many more examples from the New
Testament of the way in which Christ calls on us to
imitate his mildness. I must stress, however, that Christianity is not, in the last resort, a way of teaching or of
interpreting life. It is both of these, of course, but
ultimately and essentially it is above all a person. It is
Jesus of Nazareth, his being, his work and his life. The
Christian does not believe in a doctrine or doctrines. He
believes in Jesus Christ. The supreme law of his religious
life is a person. That is why I feel that it is important to

conclude this meditation with an outline of the mildness of Christ and the way in which the apostles experienced this in their day to day association with him.

The tenderness of Christ

The apostles began to associate with Jesus quite as a matter of course, as though they were ordinary friends. How does friendship begin? People encounter each other and, after an initial hesitation, they come closer to each other as human beings. The two disciples of John the Baptist followed Jesus nervously at first. Their master had encouraged them to do this. 'Where are you staying?' they asked him and he replied: 'Come and see'. Then they went with him and stayed with him until late that evening.

This is the way many friendships begin — a meeting, an invitation and a conversation. The hours pass and suddenly the friends notice that it has become late. After this first meeting, Jesus' disciples went about their own business again, but they saw more and more of Jesus. Almost without their noticing it, their lives became interwoven with his. Jesus was not in a hurry. He knew that friendships have to take their time. They have their own rhythm. It is one of the most striking characteristics of mild people that they give others their freedom. They never do violence to them. They are also mild in their attitude towards time. They let friendship develop at its own pace.

After the initial stage, Jesus began to work miracles in the presence of his disciples. They were also witnesses of the first controversy with the pharisees. Then came the first journey together. Jesus went up a mountain and called those whom he had chosen to be 'with him'. From then onwards, he called them his friends. He stood up for them and, despite their slowness to understand, remained faithful to them. Behind his mildness lay inner freedom and a deep peace. Only the really strong man is able to be completely without violence.

Weak people are almost always violent. Jesus was strong, never violent and above all mild. But we have to learn how to see him with fresh eyes and get rid of the image of the 'sweet Saviour' if we are to understand how mysteriously disconcerting his mildness is.

Freud was right — and, what is more, very close to the truth of the gospel — when he called the heart of the weak man a murderer's den. In our unconscious desires, we suppress people who give rise to unpleasant feelings in us. Our deep violence is hidden behind petty irritations, always knowing better than other people, constantly giving good advice and a sharply critical attitude, almost one of persecution of other people, which is not always expressed in words, but can always be felt. In our virtuous indignation, our constant suggestions for improving the world and our little humiliations imposed on ourselves and others, we waste the energy of our heart, in order to assert ourselves over others and damage them.

We can thank Freud for this self-knowledge, but he was not the first to discover it. 'Any one who hates his brother', we are told in the first letter of John, 'is a murderer' (1 Jn 3. 15) and 'You have heard that it was said to the men of old, "You shall not kill; and whoever kills shall be liable to judgment", Jesus said, 'But I say to you that everyone who is angry with his brother shall be liable to judgment" ' (Mt 5. 21-22).

If we read the gospel in this way and try to grasp the figure of Christ in the simplest events narrated in it, we shall not fail to observe how powerfully what is completely different and cannot be grasped at the purely human level breaks through in him. He surrounds his disciples, even Judas Iscariot, with an atmosphere of mildness. Judas was already moving away from him, inwardly at least, from the time of the discourse on the Bread of Life. Jesus was aware of this and pained by it, but he went on treating Judas like the others and tried every way of bringing him back. In the garden of Gethsemane, when Judas kissed him to show that he was the one whom they were seeking, Jesus received his betrayer with tenderness: 'Friend, why are you here?' We may say with truth that there was no place in Jesus' heart even for the appearance of hostility. The longer we study the gospel and look at the figure of Christ, the more overpowering is the conviction that he was no one's enemy.

Christ was the ultimate expression of perfect love in a world torn by hatred and hostility. He fought against no enemies. Indeed, it would be more correct to say that he did not fight at all. If we think carefully about his trial, we are bound to realize that he did not fight his accusers, proved nothing and disputed nothing. He simply let events take their course. His silence was not, however, the silence of weakness or despair. He was recollected, perfectly prepared and always mild.

Are we sufficiently aware of how dangerously strong tenderness can be? An apparently very ordinary sentence in Mark's gospel — 'He was in the wilderness forty days . . . with the wild beasts' (Mk 1. 13) — can give us an unexpectedly deep insight into the person of Christ, provided that we consider it in the context of the messianic kingdom that was initiated by Jesus. The hidden depths of this life with the wild animals have been indicated with great subtlety and care by the French scientist Jacques Bouillaut, who worked patiently until he succeeded in winning the friendship of eagles and other wild creatures. He tried to find the signs by which they would know that he was their friend. He worked without haste, using slow gestures and clear-cut words, directing his gaze straight into the eyes of the animal or bird. In his book, *The Eagles' Friend*, he has stressed, however, that the most important part of his work was to possess inner mildness and never to show fear — otherwise, the creatures would become restless and even attack. Mildness was strength and it, together with a complete absence of all fear clearly have a redeeming effect, and

Jacques Bouillaut — and Christ himself — have shown that this effect can also be felt even in the animal kingdom. Mildness appears in this light as a virtue of universal dimensions, the loving embrace of life that exposes itself to every experience and the deep reverence of all being even in its most humble appearance.

Let us now return to our discussion of the relationship between Christ and his apostles. Very gradually, he led them into the mystery of his inner life. He told them, for example, about the experience of being alone — his temptation in the desert and certain conversations which he conducted quite alone (the conversation with Nicodemus and the dialogue with the Samaritan woman at the well). On the other hand, the apostles knew how he never rejected individuals or large crowds of people when they came to him, even if they broke into his very short periods of peace.

It was, however, above all within the small circle of his own disciples that Jesus felt somehow more secure. It is moving to watch how these men, who were so slow to understand, were gradually initiated into the deepest mysteries of the divine life. As soon as the first difficulties began to occur, the pharisees began to persecute him and the people became puzzled by his teaching and his life, he withdrew with his disciples to Transjordania simply in order to be together with them. In the friendship and everyday intimacy of their company and in countless insignificant ways, he impressed on them the greatness of his spirit. A little child sat on his lap and this was for him an opportunity to talk about the kingdom of God. Some ordinary occurrence led him to teach them how to pray or to send them out to preach. And on their return, he would question them about their success or failure and they would be happy together.

It was above all at the Last Supper that the full depth of his love was experienced. He called his disciples his little children and his friends. He consoled them, encouraged them to love each other and showed how much he loved them in many little details. Mildness is, after all, always openness. Christ, who is mildness itself, stood then, as he stands now, in the midst of truth, creating truth. There is a certain fulness of truth which comes from the very existence of the mildness of Christ himself. In Christ there is a power of truth – he does not lie, but says positively what is true. To such an extent that this 'saying' is the medium in which the world is able to break through fully and with total conviction.

So far, then, I have mentioned three of the aspects of Christ's tenderness – its transcendent power, its complete absence of all hostility, and its openness. I should like to close this meditation with a brief outline of one final characteristic of the mildness of Christ, one that is less easy to formulate than the others. The formula 'a total openness to all suffering' does not quite cover it. Mercy is love that can be hurt and indeed has already been hurt. It is an attitude that is always careful not to cause suffering to any being – the attitude, one might almost say, of a mother to her child. But even that description does not do justice to this last characteristic of Christ's mildness, because it is basically negative and Christ's attitude here is positive.

One of the earliest titles given to Christ can perhaps point to this particular quality of his mildness. In his address to the people of Jerusalem in the third chapter of the Acts of the Apostles, Peter called Christ the 'prince of life' (Acts 3. 15). The fulness of being is in Christ, but his power is tender, sensitive and unable to harm us.

Luke describes his tenderness in a story which can surely move the hardest of hearts. Jesus was going to a little village called Nain (the evangelist calls it a town). When he was near the gate, he saw a dead man being carried out for burial. This man was the only son of his widowed mother. A great crowd was accompanying her. The Lord saw her and was at once sorry for her. ' "Do not weep", he said to her. And he came and touched the bier . . . and he said, "Young man, I say to you, arise". And the dead man sat up and began to speak. And Christ gave him back to his mother' (Lk 7. 14-17).

We can perhaps have an even deeper insight into the tenderness of Jesus in the story of the death and ressur- rection of Lazarus in the fourth gospel. The evangelist indicates in a few words how Jesus was affected by the death of this man and the suffering of his sisters: 'He was deeply moved and troubled' to see Mary weeping (Jn 11. 33). On the way to Lazarus' tomb, 'Jesus wept' (11. 35) and when they arrived at the tomb he was 'deeply moved again' (11. 38). Finally, his great love for the dead man made him call out with a powerful voice the words of life into the tomb.

We should not think of the gospel as a kind of manual of moral theology. The evangelists depict an attitude that we can never make fully our own in this life. It is quite possible that it does not matter at all to Christ that we do not succeed in our attempts to imitate him.

What he really wanted to do was to initiate a move- ment of gentleness, and to reveal to us a great panorama in front of which an entirely new and unexpected world would gradually be perceived. Mildness can, after all, be a terrifying weapon that we can use for violent purposes. It is hardly possible to define the demands made by mildness in a moral formula, but we can perhaps say that the Christian should reject malicious thoughts and actions if this is not contrary to moral principles.

We should perhaps not try to classify Christian tenderness in accordance with moral principles, because it cannot simply be neatly contained in a moral definition, a pacifist teaching or a perfect system of any kind. If we were told in the gospel: 'If you see an innocent brother being unjustly struck on one cheek, then let his attacker also strike him on the other cheek', the gospel would be making us all accomplices, sharing in the guilt. I do not deny that Christians have the right to defend themselves and to assert themselves in the name of justice. But I would insist that every blow struck against mildness is a blow against our own heart.

Quietly and in secret, turning towards the glory of the world, hope begins to grow in us. Teilhard de Chardin believed that we had reached a critical point in the evolution of the world. Our only way was to go forward in shared passion. We had to place our trust, he thought, in this evolution that came about by means of a power outside the world. And to trust in this way meant to give up everything. Were we on the way towards another, final metamorphosis? Were we, he asked, a knowledge of God in humanity? Were we moving towards the appearance of the 'theosphere'?

The story of Jonah is, I think, the most profound and at the same time the most human account of the drama that takes place throughout history between God and man. It is a divine teaching about our sanctification — our 'deification'.

Afterword

Here I simply ask: What does the story of Jonah mean for us personally? Ultimately, perhaps that we have to turn to God with another question. Or to ourselves. Inwards.

Conversion and turning inwards has been the theme of all these reflections about the story of Jonah. We are bound, in the end, to ask ourselves whether we are satisfied with our God. This may strike us at first as a very strange question, but it may be a very important and meaningful one in our lives. We can in fact turn this question in at least four different ways, although it remains basically the same, and in so doing give a good account of ourselves.

The first way of asking this question is: Am I satisfied with myself? This is really not a good way, because we are unfortunately not so created that we can ever be satisfied with ourselves. I should perhaps have used the word 'fortunately' rather than 'unfortunately' here. Man is fortunately a being who is always dissatisfied with whatever he has already gained. He was created to strive to reach the kingdom of God. He cannot be satisfied with himself.

The second way of asking is: Are others satisfied with me? Unlike the first, this is a good way of putting the question. But it is important to go further, because there is a moment in all our lives when we become aware of the fact that we can never satisfy all other people and, what is more, that we should not try to satisfy them all. What others think of us should not be our only or even our main criterion for our lives. If our lives are spent in an effort to satisfy everyone, we shall achieve very little of value.

The third way in which we can formulate this question is: Is God satisfied with me? This is, of course, something that we should ask ourselves again and again, though not to a neurotic degree. In the classroom, for example, a teacher may ask: When did Charlemagne die? And we reply at once: In 814. He asks again: Well, when did Charlemagne die? And we reply again: In 814. So he asks us again: When did Charlemagne die? Replying for the third time, we may say anything, but not 814, although it is the correct answer. God does not want us to stand proudly in front of him and tell him: 'You can be satisfied with me'. He would prefer us to be like the tax collector, who 'would not even lift his eyes to heaven, but beat his breast, saying, "God, be merciful to me a sinner!" ' (Lk 18. 13). He wants us, not our some-times self-satisfied musings about ourselves.

The fourth way of expressing this question is the best and the most fruitful: Am I satisfied with God? This is, of course, the original question and it is the only one that counts. Am I satisfied that he has created me as I am? Am I satisfied that he has given me this particular life? Am I satisfied that he does not leave me in peace? Am I satisfied that he has given me such a Redeemer, such a Church and such people in my life?

If we have really prayed a great deal and at great depth we may perhaps, almost against our own heart, be able to say: Yes, God, I am satisfied with you! I thank you that you are as you are. That would certainly be real praise and thanksgiving to offer to God: Thank you, God, for being and for being just as you are. We hope that Jonah prayed like that at the end.